POSITION CHANGING FOR VIOLIN

:KAY

Before beginning these exercises it is advisable to clean the neck of the violin with a damp cloth so that the surface of the wood is free from any dirt or perspiration which could prevent the hand from sliding smoothly up and down the instrument.

As the hand moves to 3rd Position, be careful to shift the thumb at the same time so that it occupies a similar position in relation to the fingers, as it did in 1st Position.

The change of position will produce a *glissando* at first as the finger slides over the string. This can be overcome by releasing the finger pressure slightly during the change of position, when, as the speed of the hand movement is increased, the *glissando* effect will gradually diminish.

1st FINGER MOVEMENT
A and D strings

1 — 1 means keep the finger on the string.

1. HEBRIDEAN LULLABY

2

E and A strings

2. THE FAIR ISLE

[4 bars introduction]
Allegretto

D and G strings

3. DEESIDE

[4 bars introduction]
Andantino

Position Changing for the Violin

2nd FINGER MOVEMENT

A and D strings

4. MINUET

[4 bars introduction]
Grazioso

E and A strings

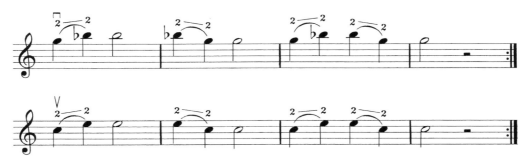

5. THE CLOWN'S DANCE

[2 bars introduction]

Allegro moderato

D and G strings

6. IN OLD MADRID

[2 bars introduction]

Andante

3rd FINGER MOVEMENT

A string

7. A SPRING MORNING

[2 bars introduction]

G string

8. EVENSONG

[4 bars introduction]

Position Changing for the Violin

6

E and D strings

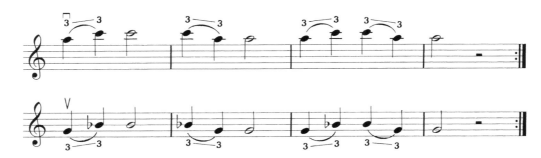

9. SNAKE ON A LADDER

[2 bars introduction]

Andantino

4th FINGER MOVEMENT
E and A strings

10. SPANISH SERENADE

[4 bars introduction]

Espressivo

D and G strings

11. IRISH LULLABY

CHANGING POSITION
From 1st Finger
to
2nd, 3rd, and 4th

The finger effecting the change of position should arrive at a guide note (♪) before the next note is played. With practice the *glissando* and guide note can be omitted.

Guide notes are not marked throughout the melodies, but should be used during each change of position.

D and G strings

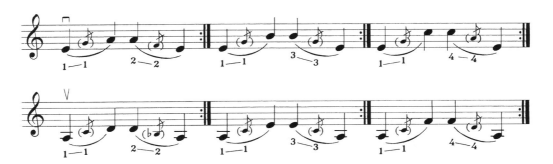

8

12. VALSE TRISTE

A and E strings

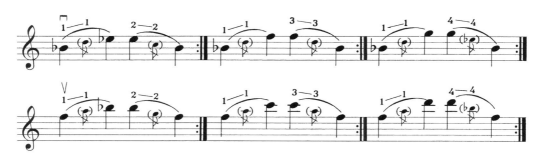

13. THE DANCING CLASS

Position Changing for the Violin

CHANGING POSITION
From 2nd and 3rd Fingers

E and A strings

14. THE TROUBADOUR'S SONG

[2 bars introduction]

Andante con moto

D and G strings

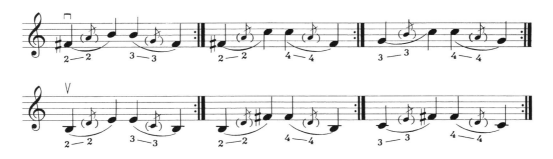

15. DANSE MACABRE

The last note of *Danse Macabre* is an Artificial Harmonic.

Stop E normally with the 1st finger, at the same time play A lightly with the pad of the 4th. This should produce a sound 2 octaves above the stopped note E.

⁴∘ HARMONICS ⁴∘

There are two types of harmonics playable on the violin. One is a NATURAL harmonic and the other ARTIFICIAL.

The following harmonics are natural, and are played half way up the string with the pad of the little finger.

Keep the left hand in 3rd Position and extend the fourth finger so that it rests lightly on the string. The violin will produce a flute-like note which is rather plaintive in sound.

16. REVEILLE
Play STACCATO notes OFF THE STRING in L.H. bow.

17. ON PARADE
Play STACCATO in U.H. bow.

18. TYROLEAN AIR

19. REVERIE

MORE GUIDE NOTES

The following changes of position are frequently used by violinists. A good player never allows the left hand to leap from one position to another, unless it entails a move from an open string to a note in a higher position, or vice versa.

Remember always to use a GUIDE NOTE when effecting a position change, and avoid any intermediate sound between changes of position.

A and E strings

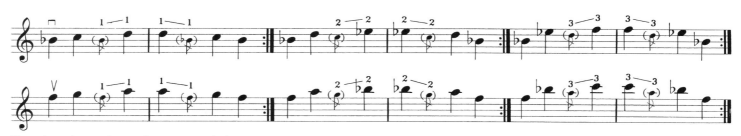

Practise also using a bow to each bar.

20. BUTTERFLIES

D and G strings

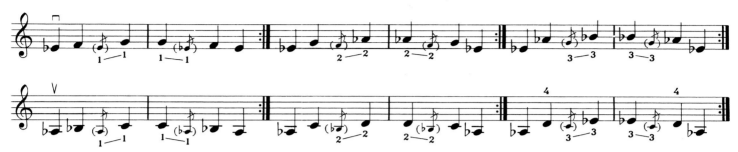

Practise also using a bow to each bar.

21. THE TENOR AND THE BASS

[2 bars introduction]

Allegro giocoso

The following melody introduces changes of position across the strings. Keep the fingers down where indicated and this will prevent any tendency to leap from one string to another.

22. WALTZING

[4 bars introduction]

Moderato

Position Changing for the Violin

Processed and printed by
Halstan & Co. Ltd., Amersham, Bucks., England

OXFORD UNIVERSITY PRESS

OXFORD MUSIC for violin includes:

J. S. Bach	*arr. Grace*	Jesu, joy of man's desiring
	arr. Forbes	Sheep may safely graze
Kathy and David Blackwell		Fiddle Time:
		Starters, Joggers, Runners, Scales
Jan Dobbins		Strings in Step, Books 1 and 2
Watson Forbes		Classical and Romantic Pieces for Violin, Books 1–4
G. F. Handel		Arrival of the Queen of Sheba
Neil Mackay		Position Changing for the Violin
Palmer and Best		Twenty Tunes for Beginners
Doreen Smith		Violin Sight-Reading, Books 1 and 2

OXFORD
UNIVERSITY PRESS

www.oup.com

ISBN 978-0-19-357653-7

9 780193 576537